# FIRST EDITION

D1637146

# I'd Rather Love You Than Be Your Friend

## 30 plus one modern proverbs that reveal the truth of God in life's moments

## JEREMIAH AREVALO

I'd Rather Love You Than Be Your Friend: 30 plus one modern proverbs that reveal the truth of God in life's moments

# Preface

I, Jeremiah Arevalo, would like to first address heaven and give the God of Abraham, Isaac, and Jacob glory for this book! Jesus has turned my impossible into the possible as well as made my crooked straight. Thank you, Lord! Secondly, I would like to address the earth and dedicate this book to my parents, who are also my pastors, James Arevalo D.D. and Dominga Arevalo. Without their love and dedication, I would have never come to know the Lord. Observing their words and deeds my entire life has filled me with divine treasure. I became inspired to read the Holy Bible and learn the ways of the Lord. The inspiration for the format of this book came through a common personal devotional, which is to read a Proverb and Psalm every day. Specifically, Proverbs has thirty-one chapters so I read one a day until I complete a month. That is why this book has thirty-one sayings, one for every day of the month. Years of daily mediation together with trials of fire have forged the sayings of this book. I hope to help people understand the truth and see the beauty of life. Jesus is the truth and Jesus is the beauty! My heart's longing is to hear a stranger quote me. Thank you for picking this book!

# 1. I'd rather love you than be your friend

At first, the above seems like a paradox, an odd statement with no place. Yet, so often this is love. A struggle between happy and hurt, accepting and rejecting, and truth and lies. At the end of the day, it all boils down to faith, with us hoping we made the best decision for others and ourselves. The saying here came to me when I was young in the Lord. When I came to the knowledge of the truth, I began to preach the truth. I realized that for most people the Gospel of Jesus Christ is a deal-breaker for friendship. If I spoke about the weather, work, family, and society there would be laughter, smiles, and good vibes. The moment I introduced Jesus is the moment I became ex-communicated or simply put, the outcast. You are not cool anymore, nor are you considered a friend. I would think to myself that I am doing my best to love this person, and who would not want an honest friend. The truth of this saying became confirmed again and again because it happened repeatedly with different people and at different places. What is that truth? The world's perception of a friend is not based on love. Sure, on the surface, the world's perception has the appearance of love because two people share common beliefs, make each other feel good, and are a shoulder at times to lean on, but all these things are based on conditions. If conditions are broken so is the friendship. One of the Greek words for love is agape, which means unconditional love. Basically, you love someone even when they do not love back. The world does not do this, it gives gifts to those who give them gifts back. When you love someone, you give that someone Jesus, who is love. Human nature cannot handle this love because this love is holy. Most people live in human nature. Therefore, if you preach Jesus, you will be rejected even though you are loving them. I know what it is to be the rejector as well. My Pastors, also known as my parents, would give me Jesus and I rebelled against them for it. Time and time again I chose evil relationships over them. Thanks be to God that my parents were faithful and absorbed my mistreatment because it saved my soul! Another truth that I have seen is that when the rejector is visited by evil, the person who preached Jesus is the person they reach out to for help. So, be strong in this struggle to love, for God is always rejected first and He understands our pain. What a mighty God we serve!

**Romans 5:8 (KJV) But God commendeth his love toward us, in that, while we were yet sinners, Christ died for us.**

**Luke 6:32 (KJV) For if ye love them which love you, what thank have ye? for sinners also love those that love them.**

**John 15:18 (KJV) If the world hate you, ye know that it hated me before it hated you.**

**Matthew 5:44 (KJV) But I say unto you, Love your enemies, bless them that curse you, do good to them that hate you, and pray for them which despitefully use you, and persecute you**

## 2. Just because you have common ground with someone does not mean it is good soil

I worked in sales before and a general tactic taught was to find common ground. The reason for doing so was to connect with the customer to become trustworthy. Then the customer would be more inclined to listen to you. The main goal for sales was to make a sale. People have different motives for connecting with you. God understands this all too well and provides warnings for this behavior. There are good relationships and there are bad relationships. What determines if something is good or bad? It is not what, it is who, Jesus. It is our responsibility to make righteous judgments before entering courtship, friendship, and business. Essentially, anything that binds you with a commitment to another person that will affect testimony and salvation must be on holy terms. Relationships are a matter of life and death. I am sure that each of us can think of an unhealthy relationship that we have been in or seen someone else in. I have fallen victim to connecting with a person and thinking it is from God. I mean, things were popping off like New Year's Day because we had so much in common (at least in the small time we were getting to know each other), but at the same time, small red flags were telling me this was not right. I could feel my heart justifying and burying the red flags, yet my spirit would not let me forget. I had to remind myself that before Christ, emotions and different beliefs dictated my decisions. Now, my decisions are inspired and influenced by the Spirit with the support of the Holy Scriptures. When I recalled this truth, I tested the relationship in the Spirit and it certainly failed to be from God. Thank God it was right on time for no one was wounded in the soul! I know that the Lord saved me and the other person from much evil conflict. Praise be to the Lord for His guidance! It is not about the common ground. It is about the higher ground. A good relationship should bear fruit unto the Lord. This begins in the soil where we should be close to humbly and prayerfully.

**2 Corinthians 6:14 (KJV) Be ye not unequally yoked together with unbelievers: for what fellowship hath righteousness with unrighteousness? and what communion hath light with darkness?**

**Proverbs 28:26 (KJV) He that trusteth in his own heart is a fool: but whoso walketh wisely, he shall be delivered.**

**Proverbs 13:20 (KJV) He that walketh with wise men shall be wise: but a companion of fools shall be destroyed.**

**1 John 4:1 (KJV) Beloved, believe not every spirit, but try the spirits whether they are of God: because many false prophets are gone out into the world.**

# 3. If you do not work to do good, then you will work to do evil

In this world, there is a price for everything. When we decide to be lazy, idle, and sluggish then consequences will certainly overtake us. It sure feels good to do no work and to sleep in, but this is a lifestyle that cannot be maintained. This truth applies to the physical and spiritual realm. I recall in my younger years not being able to hold a job and just sleeping most of the day. Of course, this routine was enabled by a guardian, but it was by design. It kept me dependent and a willing participant in my guardian's evil requests as well as a pawn in my guardian's plans to hurt others. So, not being a productive worker led me to be a slave to an evil puppet master. Be very careful with individuals who support your temporary indulgences over your permanent good! Another perspective in this scenario of being a lazy person is self-esteem. When you are not accomplishing anything, you feel worthless and others, like family and friends, know your situation so it becomes dishonorable. Some people get swallowed whole by the evil and their conscious becomes seared so much that they don't care about their reputation. At that point, you then become a sad situation with people shaking their heads at you. If the situation persists long enough then you become a joke and a saying i.e. "You're doing a (Insert Name)." Now, with all this time on a lazy person's hands mischief is usually the filler. Then comes the hanging out with the foolish, perhaps gangs and thieves, which leads to crime and jail. The hole gets wider and deeper, and the pressures of evil persist.

In prison, survival is vital, and the options are minimal. I have seen people choose prison gangs, which led to them being told what to do by their higher-ups. So, now they are putting in work, evil work, like physically assaulting people, selling drugs, and unmentionable behaviors. All of this because a person decided not to work at good. Please understand that the more you give to human nature, the more it takes from your soul. There is no neutral ground. You either go forward or you go backward. The devil knows this and lurks to pounce on the opportunity. The opportunity to make you a worker for hell. Praise be to God that He provides strength for those willing to do good!

**Proverbs 10:5 (KJV) He that gathereth in summer is a wise son: but he that sleepeth in harvest is a son that causeth shame**

**Proverbs 12:11 (KJV) He that tilleth his land shall be satisfied with bread: but he that followeth vain persons is void of understanding.**

**Proverbs 12:24 (KJV) The hand of the diligent shall bear rule: but the slothful shall be under tribute.**

**Philippians 2:13 (KJV) For it is God which worketh in you both to will and to do of his good pleasure.**

## 4. The world may call me names and accuse me, but none of it will enter heaven

One of the meanings of the name Satan is the accuser. Satan accuses to taint or stain your name, which is connected to your reputation, your honor, and ultimately your testimony. Therefore, to mock God, disprove faith, and destroy souls Satan requests trials to sift us as wheat or separate us from God. The Bible says that Satan is the god of this world so it should not be troubling that the world is going to behave like its god and accuse also. Their tongue shoots off like a machine gun with hateful names! Name-calling is attempting to characterize who you are, show what you represent, and charge you with wrongdoing. There are times when a believer takes an accusation as a defendant when the believer should take the accusation as a witness. If we stay in Christ, there is no more condemnation. We must ask ourselves, what is the point of the accusation? It is to prove whether our testimony is real or fake, truth or false. Satan does not want real testimonies that support that Jesus is the Way, the Truth, and the Life. Further, Satan does not want to reveal that he exists as well. The danger in this world is that truth can be turned into a lie and a lie can be turned into truth. Though, it is all earthly perception, for there is only absolute truth in the spiritual realm. The spiritual realm is the supreme reality. It is hurtful and tiresome when the world tarnishes us and heaps loads of dirt upon us. Absorb the nutrients of the dirt, seek the light, and humbly break through the surface like a seed becoming a tree! If a person believes a lie about you then they would not believe the truth in general. That person either wants you to be like them or to be beneath them. So, do not take the accusation personally, but pray for the accuser to come to the knowledge of the truth. Then this would allow them to see the real you. Jesus always depended upon God to be His judge, which is why the world was puzzled at His silence. Do you ever see dirt on the top of trees? If you continue in healthy growth and maturity the dirt will not stick! What matters is what the Judge, our Heavenly Father, says and seek only His affirmation. After we have endured, God will call us by our real name in heaven! Offer praise to our glorious King of Kings!

**Revelation 12:9,10 (KJV) And the great dragon was cast out, that old serpent, called the Devil, and Satan, which deceiveth the whole world: he was cast out into the earth, and his angels were cast out with him. 10 And I heard a loud voice saying in heaven, Now is come salvation, and strength, and the kingdom of our God, and the power of his Christ: for the accuser of our brethren is cast down, which accused them before our God day and night.**

**Mark 15:3 (KJV) And the chief priests accused him of many things: but he answered nothing.**

**Revelation 2:17 (KJV) He that hath an ear, let him hear what the Spirit saith unto the churches; To him that overcometh will I give to eat of the hidden manna, and will give him a white stone, and in the stone a new name written, which no man knoweth saving he that receiveth it.**

# 5. When you pray, God intervenes so you do not become the prey

The Holy Scriptures state that Jesus fell on his face and prayed. The physical act of prayer places one's body in a surrender position. To the world, this is a weak idea with many secular leaders stating that they would rather die than bend their knees. In war, when the opponent surrenders, he either has hands in the air, on knees or both. This is a concession to power. In other words, a person surrenders to the will of another. The war for souls began when the serpent presented the temptation to Adam and Eve. Man lost the beginning round, but Jesus won the last round so we must decide who we apply to our soul. Are we going to be the first Adam or the last Adam? Do we continue in the human nature passed on or do we overcome and take on Christ's nature? Continuing in human nature means you subject yourself to the serpent's temptations. Overcoming is to take the example of Jesus who surrendered his body to the Spirit's power. Jesus was obedient to the Father and lived spiritually, which included the basis for a spiritual relationship, prayer. Do you think people would experience love or make any advancement without communication? I certainly know man would not. How do we expect to experience God's love and power without prayer? Prayer is the main line of communication with our Creator. It breaths in the Spirit and breaths out the flesh or human nature, which is the main predator. You come face to face with your weakness with admittance and humbleness, surrendering your limits to the unlimited source, Jesus. God does not turn away a broken spirit that pleas to be made whole in truth and righteousness. The moment that prayer is forsaken is the moment a soul shows up on the devil's radar and demons take to their battle stations. The curse of the serpent is to feed off the dust of the earth. Man's flesh is made from the dust of the earth. Remaining in the flesh will feed the enemy. His fangs sunk in pumping venom with some just being wounded and others losing their lives. The flesh's most dreaded act is to pray. It's a whirlwind of thoughts and emotions as the flesh and the devil attempt to stop your prayer. Notice that I said attempt because they can try, but you decide to be stopped or not! What are you going to do?

**Isaiah 56:7 (KJV) Even them will I bring to my holy mountain, and make them joyful in my house of prayer: their burnt offerings and their sacrifices shall be accepted upon mine altar; for mine house shall be called an house of prayer for all people.**

**Acts 6:4 (KJV) But we will give ourselves continually to prayer, and to the ministry of the word.**

**Matthew 26:41 (KJV) Watch and pray, that ye enter not into temptation: the spirit indeed is willing, but the flesh is weak.**

**Luke 22:44 (KJV) And being in an agony he (Jesus) prayed more earnestly: and his sweat was as it were great drops of blood falling down to the ground**

## 6. If God showed me 1/10 of what I was going to go through, I would not have done it. Since God in His wisdom gave daily, He deserves the perfect 10!

One of the most beautiful displays of strength and love is that Jesus foresaw His sacrifice on the cross, yet He chose to still endure the shame and pain. I recall as a child that the expectation of a spanking was just as bad and sometimes worse than the spanking itself. Even though I did wrong, I still attempted to get out of the punishment. One time I thought I got smart and I decided to put towels to pad my bottom to take the blows of the spanking. The first licks came and I did not feel it, so I had to put on a show, fake tears and all. Eventually, my father caught on and I got it worse. If I would have succeeded in my little stunt, I am sure that bigger stunts would have resulted. I was attempting to escape the pain and correction. Often our perception of pain and suffering is based upon the good and bad we have done, but what about the evil inside that needs to be purged out? Our behavior reveals a condition, and it is always a heart condition. There are issues in our hearts that we don't even know exist. Impatience left the body when the patient trial was upon us. Unforgiveness left the heart when we became in need of forgiveness. Love filled our soul when the light at the end of the tunnel revealed what and why we went through it. Strive to reach the light! God, knowing our human nature gently leads us into suffering and tribulations. Firstly, He knows what we can handle and administers accordingly. Secondly, God encourages and cautions to prepare for battles. It is like wounds on the left and healing on the right. God's love overpowers the hate, God's light overpowers the dark! God's perfect intervention provides us with a perfect balance of forging our soul in righteousness without breaking us. If God just thrust my battles upon me, I know I would not be standing. If God showed me it all, I would not even make it to the starting line. Since the Lord does what He does marvelously, I can stand through it all! So, what is the perfect 10 God deserves from us out of every trial? 1) Praise 2) Grateful Heart 3) Pure Acceptance 4) Trust 5) Faithfulness 6) Teachable Spirit 7) Overcome in Righteousness 8) Patient Endurance 9) Testimony 10) Worship. To the Glory of God!

**Hebrews 12:2 (KJV) Looking unto Jesus the author and finisher of our faith; who for the joy that was set before him endured the cross, despising the shame, and is set down at the right hand of the throne of God.**

**1 Corinthians 10:13 (KJV) There hath no temptation taken you but such as is common to man: but God is faithful, who will not suffer you to be tempted above that ye are able; but will with the temptation also make a way to escape, that ye may be able to bear it.**

**Romans 5: 3,4 (KJV) And not only so, but we glory in tribulations also: knowing that tribulation worketh patience; 4 And patience, experience; and experience, hope:**

## 7. In the Lord, the bad happens for the good, and the good happens for the good!

There are several decisions we made that we could agree were not the best and caused us or others harm. A decision as a sinner and out of the will of God is like a bomb causing irreversible destruction to its target and surroundings. A decision as a believer and out of the will of God is like a house demolition. It is controlled chaos with an ability to rebuild and to rebuild better. Now, this is for the bad/evil that results from us as believers because we allowed more flesh into our walk instead of being led by the spirit. Though, we need to be careful how far we go in the flesh for we can reach the point of being back in sin and thus back to the bomb scenario. There is bad that happens to us that did not originate from us so to speak. For example, Job in the Holy Bible was requested by Satan to have his faith tested. Job's friends were insistent that Job sinned for this bad to be upon him. That was not the case and Job's friends were rebuked by God for saying so. For a better understanding of what and why a trial is upon us, my Pastor, Dominga Arevalo, says this, "A trial that could have been prevented comes from us, and a trial that could not have been prevented comes from the Lord." If we truly have faith in God, then we have faith in who He is, a perfect, holy, and righteous Being. A perfect Being cannot make mistakes so whatever trial at hand that did not come by our hand is good. This is hard to grasp because good is used so loosely in society. Good means moral excellence. Trials teach us to be morally excellent to melt away the disobedient layers of the flesh. When the trial happens by our hand God is just and He will not allow us to be overwhelmed, but we need to have sincere convictions about repenting. Sincere repentance allows our spiritual eyes to be opened by the Lord to see the error of our ways. Then we can build upon a stronger foundation and be a shelter for ourselves and others. So, stay in God even if we stepped out of His will a bit. Jump back in, pray, and push forward! When good is upon us, let us not slip into slack. The good happens because that is just who God is toward us. The good also happens to reward good behavior such as obeying godly principles. Now, we cannot keep the good all to ourselves for God wants to allow us to be godly, or just like Him, by blessing our neighbor. The blessings do not overflow to be wasted on the ground. Heaven forbids! Reach out and bless someone today! Hallelujah!

**2 Corinthians 2:14 (KJV) Now thanks be unto God, which always causeth us to triumph in Christ, and maketh manifest the savour of his knowledge by us in every place.**

**Romans 8:28 (KJV) And we know that all things work together for good to them that love God, to them who are the called according to his purpose.**

**1 Timothy 6:18,19 (KJV) That they do good, that they be rich in good works, ready to distribute, willing to communicate; 19 Laying up in store for themselves a good foundation against the time to come, that they may lay hold on eternal life.**

## 8. Every time Jesus is present, but it is up to us to be in His presence

God helps us all, the sinners and the saints, from the first breath to the last breath. This is the unconditional love that pours from our Creator's nature. How much love we experience is up to us? For example, a man has two daughters, one rebellious and one obedient, and both live with the man. As a father, the man cares for his children by providing food, shelter, and around-the-clock love. For the rebellious daughter, she has convinced herself with the help of liars that love is somewhere else. The rebellious daughter runs away and experiences all manner of suffering in the world yet continues to swallow spoonfuls of lies. The obedient daughter stays in the presence of her father and enjoys all benefits. The father has no choice, but to focus his love on who is near him. The father loves the rebellious daughter the best and only way he can, by praying for her return and by remaining with open arms. Even though his arms hurt from remaining open God places His arms in support of the father. The physical father is present, but the rebellious daughter is not in his presence. So it is with God's creation, some rebellious and some obedient, receiving their amount of presence accordingly. Some say, well, the physical father is limited and cannot be everywhere, but God can be everywhere so why can't the rebellious be in the presence of God the same way as the obedient? Yes, God is everywhere, but He cannot be near sin and rebellion. If God got near to sin this would taint His nature. Therefore, Jesus says, come to me, though He leads us in the process. Upon returning to Jesus there is repentance, sincerity, truth, acceptance, and cleansing. Do you know what supports the arms of God to remain open even though His arms are weary? It is the cross of Christ, the demonstration of love! Once a sinner repents and comes into the arms of Jesus then the saint can experience the warmth and full joy of the presence (Yes, the change is that fast). Do not run away from God, instead run to God and as soon as you take your sincere steps, God will run to you!

**Acts 17:27 (KJV) That they should seek the Lord, if haply they might feel after him, and find him, though he be not far from every one of us:**

**1 Samuel 15:23 (KJV) For rebellion is as the sin of witchcraft, and stubbornness is as iniquity and idolatry. Because thou hast rejected the word of the Lord, he hath also rejected thee from being king.**

**Psalm 145:18 (KJV) The Lord is nigh unto all them that call upon him, to all that call upon him in truth.**

**Psalm 16:11 (KJV) Thou wilt shew me the path of life: in thy presence is fulness of joy; at thy right hand there are pleasures for evermore.**

## 9. The devil treats you well and fattens you up, ONLY to eat you

Hansel and Gretel may be a fairy tale, but where did the inspiration of such a story originate? It is simple to see that in this world there are predators who play a nice role to their victims. Here are some scenarios which reveal the blueprints of the devil. Worldly famous entertainers boast of their luxurious lifestyles and project the message, "Look at me, you should want what I have." Their entertainment makes you feel good and at times helps you get through something, but it is nothing more than swallowing water while drowning. Does all their fame and riches have no cost? They will not tell you how miserable they are with many people telling them what to do, when to do it, and how to do it. Further, they have very limited privacy. The rich and famous are swallowed up by their very pleasures and often are addicted to drugs and alcohol. Further, they are sorrowful and lose their lives at an early age. In the life to come their destination will likely be hell, for they did not have room for God in their lives and they remained unrepentant. Hell will eat and swallow them for it is never satisfied. So, the devil grants the fame, riches, pleasures, and treats them well (well with a price still), but it is for a hellish demise for them and their followers. Then there is this scenario, an enticing and lustful beautiful woman or handsome man. Seducing and luring with the appeal of happiness. At first, the seducers demonstrate selfless behavior like paying for meals, getting in good with family, and knowing the smallest of details of a person's every want. This is nothing more than a predator stalking its prey and studying its every move to devour it without any harm to itself. At times, glimpses of their motives are seen in a fit of anger or peculiar situation, but quickly the enticers talk it away. Due to the weakness of seeking false love, loneliness, and fulfillment of other desires, they are quickly forgiven. The game resumes and with every moment the enticers are earning more and more trust and love. The victim at the moment describes the game as being breathtaking, but the situation is more like a boa constrictor tightening and taking your breath with every squeeze. As soon as the enticers know that your heart belongs to them that is when the true colors come out and hell begins to feast. Some have lost property, lives, and their very soul to the above scenarios. Beware, feeling good and the actual good can be at odds with one another. Jesus treats you well so that you can eat with Him forever in love, joy, and peace! Thank you, Jesus!

**Matthew 19:24 (KJV) And again I say unto you, It is easier for a camel to go through the eye of a needle, than for a rich man to enter into the kingdom of God.**

**Proverbs 7:21,22 (KJV) With her much fair speech she caused him to yield, with the flattering of her lips she forced him. 22 He goeth after her straightway, as an ox goeth to the slaughter, or as a fool to the correction of the stocks**

**Luke 4:6 (KJV) And the devil said unto him, All this power will I give thee, and the glory of them: for that is delivered unto me; and to whomsoever I will I give it.**

# 10. Disobedience is a gateway sin

"I haven't killed anybody," "I don't drink beer or smoke," and "I don't do drugs," are the quotes of individuals justifying themselves into being good people. These sins by the way are just icing on the sin cake and people have different icings at times. Evil behavior like drunkenness and getting high on drugs comes from the condition of human nature, which is disobedient and sinful. Now, human nature also known as the flesh, is the substance, the cake so to speak. Let us examine what happened in the garden of Eden. Did Adam and Eve kill anybody (though sin does bring death)? No. What was so horrible that Adam and Eve were kicked out of the garden of Eden and had to die? Disobedience. God commanded (spoken Word) Adam and Eve to not eat from the tree of the knowledge of good and evil. God's Word is love, is pure, is holy, and is good, so the trespass of Adam and Eve was against these, against Him. God's nature, God's condition is love, and love is holiness and righteousness. God's Word and nature are one, both never contradicting one another. Just like two parallel lines will go on forever, so will God's nature and Word! A relationship with God must be on the terms of love. For example, what type of marriage relationship is healthy when one spouse commits adultery against another spouse? One spouse can choose to forgive, but to remain together is contingent upon the adultery not happening again. Love expressed through faithfulness in this scenario is the determinant for a healthy relationship so the relationship can produce good and more love. Love never fails, so when a relationship fails it is because love has been removed. Therefore, Adam and Eve could not remain with God because disobedience removed love from the relationship. From disobedience came the sinful nature and all manner of sins. Therefore, we must be born-again (spiritually), to get out of the disobedient nature and into the obedient nature. An obedient nature heeds to the Word of God and strives to perfect itself in love. A disobedient nature seeks to please itself according to self's interpretations of love. Anything other than the Word of God is lies, hate, and unholiness. The condition of the fallen nature of man cannot be trusted. Man's history should serve as a perfect example of the evil that man's nature can produce. Disobeying love opens the gates to sin, hate, and the chaos that follows. Rebuke the flesh by the blood of the Lamb of God! God deserves our obedience!

**Psalm 51:5 (KJV) Behold, I was shapen in iniquity; and in sin did my mother conceive me.**

**Romans 8:8 (KJV) So then they that are in the flesh cannot please God.**

**Romans 5:19 (KJV) For as by one man's disobedience many were made sinners, so by the obedience of one shall many be made righteous.**

**John 14:15 (KJV) If ye love me, keep my commandments.**

## 11. God's humbleness is higher than man's pride. Fear the Lord!

Have you ever known a giant person, yet they are just a big teddy bear? You know that at any moment this person could crush another person, but they are gentle and kind. This giant person deserves double respect. Since the capability to bully is there, yet this person chooses to be large in kindness! God is all-powerful and at any moment His enemies can be devoured. What does God choose to do? He chooses to be slow to anger, compassionate, and the God of many chances. This truly amazes me! Though man hates, rebels, and is swollen with pride, God's love dictates His will toward us. Did you catch that? God's love is always working for us so don't get confused during suffering. God is up and we are down, still we humans act like we are up, and He is down. God looks down at us, but God does not look down on us. Even more so, God came down, humbled Himself as defenseless as a baby. Then as a child, Jesus taught about His Father's kingdom. Imagine it, God was a child pleading with His creation to follow Him into life in all meekness and vulnerability. How can we trample on such a beautiful expression of love from our Heavenly Father? Into adulthood, Jesus continued showing the world truth and the representation of God the Father with glorious displays of power in kindness. Jesus did not condemn a single soul. He preached repentance so man would not stay in their sin so that He could save them. Evil and pride are dominating the earth. This domination will be short-lived and the only reason it flourishes is due to the patience of God who wants more souls to repent before the judgment. There is no evil act that goes overlooked. Either the penalty of that evil is paid by the blood of Jesus or by our blood. The cup of iniquity is being filled and it will pour over one day unleashing wrath never experienced before on earth. The wrath will continue into eternity. Love will defeat hate, peace will defeat violence, and humbleness will defeat pride. When Jesus ascended into heaven from earth, He said He would return in the same way, but understand that Jesus will be more than just Savior. Jesus will be the King of Kings! A ruler to establish righteousness and peace! Pride will be defeated forever! More love, more power, more of you Lord!

**Luke 2:42,47 And when he (Jesus) was twelve years old, they went up to Jerusalem after the custom of the feast.47 And all that heard him (Jesus) were astonished at his understanding and answers.**

**Matthew 21:42,44 (KJV) Jesus saith unto them, Did ye never read in the scriptures, The stone which the builders rejected, the same is become the head of the corner: this is the Lord's doing, and it is marvellous in our eyes? 44 And whosoever shall fall on this stone shall be broken: but on whomsoever it shall fall, it will grind him to powder.**

## 12. People say the devil does not sleep, but when you pray and believe you give that fool a nap!

So much credit is given to the enemy. The enemy is the devil. Satan is the leech of the universe who only gets fed by a willing host. He is the greatest con of all time for he has gained all his power by gift. Every position, angle, and hold has come by way of a person giving it willingly. Speaking of which, the devil is not God's equal nor is he stronger than truth, righteousness, and salvation. Satan must ask permission from God for every attack, trial, and tribulation. The statement that the devil does not sleep grants divine qualities to this fool. The devil can only come in seasons or short periods. Never lay down to evil and let it reign in your house, in your space at work, or daily walk. We have the power in the name of Jesus to rebuke the enemy back to hell. We must show society, our children, and others that evil has a limit and that God is unlimited. In this world, evil seems to continue limitlessly, but this is because the world submits to the prince of darkness's reign. A Christian through the blood of Jesus knocks that crown off. Prayer and belief are the keys! Keeping in the presence of God and allowing for the presence of God to move on others is a dynamic of prayer. Believing also moves our Lord to action because belief is obedience to His promises! Where the presence of the Lord is there is freedom and liberty! That means the chains and plans of evil are broken. Daniel in the Bible was prayed-up, which strengthened his belief so when he was thrown into the den of hungry lions the presence of God was there and closed the mouths of the lions. I am sure Daniel used the lions as a pillow through the night. By the way, Daniel saw the lions before the lions saw him, but he submitted to God anyway. In the morning Daniel was removed from the den and the plan of evil failed. Think of this, Satan used willing helpers, who were presidents and princes in King Darius' kingdom, to attack Daniel. Those helpers with their families were thrown into the lion's den and were consumed. The plot to harm Daniel was turned on them instead. Daniel's act of courage and faith changed a whole government as well as laid the foundation for religious freedom doctrines in future secular governments. So, when the devil sought to put Daniel to sleep, Daniel through prayer and belief in God put the devil to sleep in more ways than one! Is there a witness? Let the church say Amen!

**Ephesians 4:27 (KJV) Neither give place to the devil.**

**Matthew 17:21 (KJV) Howbeit this kind goeth not out but by prayer and fasting.**

**Luke 4:13 (KJV) And when the devil had ended all the temptation, he departed from him for a season.**

**John 17:15 (KJV) I pray not that thou shouldest take them out of the world, but that thou shouldest keep them from the evil.**

# 13. Aeronautics looks to the bird and the bird looks to God

Aeronautics is the study of flight or simply put, making things fly. Mankind already walks on the ground and occasionally gets to higher ground from hills and mountains, however, man desires to go higher. A person desires to disconnect from the ground and soar. What do you suppose is the inspiration? I believe it is what has always flown above man's head, birds. These creatures have in their bodies the mastery of physics, gravity, and wind. A bird is not an intelligent being thus the phrase, "bird brain." The intelligence of the bird is in what it is, a marvel of nature and a challenger of the law of gravity. A bird can fly due to several factors. The bird has light bones, able legs for lift-off, wind-piercing wings, and feathers that become propelled with air. If the bird inspired a person to fly, who inspired the bird to fly? God, who is seated in the Highest! A bird is a creature and God is the Creator! What else can we learn from birds? How about to look up! Isn't it peculiar that a defeated person's body will appear slouched and their gaze down? On the other hand, a person who has won will have their body stretched to the highest limit with hands up. Inside of us, a win is up, and a loss is down. I have heard a preacher say, when you look down you see, "de-feet." Well, who resides below, Satan. That is why he is a defeated foe. The Word says to look to the hills from where our help comes! When a person took to the skies in flight, he conquered the limitations of gravity and at the same time maximized the science of air. Where man fails is that he does not look higher than the bird. It is like a person who shops at the grocery store and can't see past the food shelves to see that the food came from the earth through a beautiful process. A process that includes a balance of man working the land and God providing the necessities, like rain, for increase. Man is also flawed in that he cannot conqueror sin, but sin was conquered for us by Jesus! Jesus was placed off the ground, between heaven and earth. Just as the bird is lifted high for us to see flight, so the cross was lifted high for us to see our loving God! If we accept Jesus, we will overcome the limitations of the sinful nature and maximize on grace. Then prepare to meet the Lord in the air! Hallelujah!

**Genesis 1:20 (KJV) And God said, Let the waters bring forth abundantly the moving creature that hath life, and fowl that may fly above the earth in the open firmament of heaven.**

**Job 12:7 (KJV) But ask now the beasts, and they shall teach thee; and the fowls of the air, and they shall tell thee:**

**Matthew 10:29 (KJV) Are not two sparrows sold for a farthing? and one of them shall not fall on the ground without your Father.**

**Psalm 124:7 (KJV) Our soul is escaped as a bird out of the snare of the fowlers: the snare is broken, and we are escaped.**

## 14. You do not have a problem; you just have a topic for prayer

Any problem will be stressful and demand energy from us, although how the stress will impact us is up to us. News media outlets certainly reveal to us how society buckles under the pressure often with deadly consequences. Death is not in God's plan. Life has always been the Lord our God's purpose. Why then do we have stress, issues, problems, trials, pressures, and deadly consequences? It is due to sin, the life-taker of man. When man stepped out of the garden of Eden, he stepped on thorns and into a world against him. Though people and things in this world harm us, God still heals us. So, in every circumstance we must seek the healer. There is negative stress and positive stress. For example, stress and resistance on the body's muscles also called exercise, which causes the muscles to break down will then rebuild or heal as stronger muscles. You will feel the soreness or pain for a few days, but rest assured you will heal stronger! Muscles are not the only things to benefit as a result of exercise for organs, bones, and vascular systems benefit as well. Another key benefit of exercise is that it influences the mind to be healthy. An example of negative stress would be the breaking of a bone, which has no real benefit for the body. When a problem arises, we must have the goal to become stronger and not broken, but the target is not the body, it is the spirit. Prayer allows for God to be for us and if God is for us then nothing can be against us. Speaking to God in the Holy Ghost works out the spirit, renews the mind, and provides strength for the battle.

Remember, Jesus prayed so hard that his sweat was like drops of blood. Understand that problems are a tool for breaking down our pride and for the purging of dependence on ourselves. If we stay in fellowship with God by the mainline of prayer through the problem, then what will rebuild or heal is humble, mature, and spiritually strong. When a person sees that their physical strength is diminishing, feeling sluggish, or that they cannot last as long in an activity, then the usual phrase that would follow is that "It's gym time!" If you are facing a problem that has you depleted, perplexed, or influences you to surrender to temptation, then tell yourself, "It's prayer time!" Then go pray. Praying is talking with God and problems are just a topic in that talk. God is the best at answering! Be exalted Lord!

**Job 5:7 (KJV) Yet man is born unto trouble, as the sparks fly upward.**

**Luke 22:44 (KJV) And being in an agony he prayed more earnestly: and his sweat was as it were great drops of blood falling down to the ground.**

**Jude 1:20 (KJV) But ye, beloved, building up yourselves on your most holy faith, praying in the Holy Ghost**

**2 Corinthians 12:10 (KJV) Therefore I take pleasure in infirmities, in reproaches, in necessities, in persecutions, in distresses for Christ's sake: for when I am weak, then am I strong.**

## 15. Be an open good book, if not, you risk being the fourth leg on a couch

Share yourself with the world, the good that is and not the evil. You see, we must not be any book, we must be the very Word of God! Everyone advertises their beliefs in one way or another. Every song, philosophy, political choice, social taboo, et cetera is projecting a "do" and a "do not." Notice, that what is opposite of the Word of God is the world's dominant message. Why? Evil does its best to close the Word of God. The Word of God is intended to be opened, then read, and then acted upon. The library of heaven sent the Word of God into the world so souls may know God. Jesus fulfilled every letter of the law and said that one jot shall not be removed until it is fulfilled. That is how open God is because He gave us the message through the prophets, scriptures, and in Himself. Now, He commands us to be the messengers. Societies have their messages, which are doctrines of devils, for appeasing or satisfying the flesh's desires. Evil is given an intellectual stamp of approval. For example, the killing of babies, abortion, is intellectualized as being a woman's right to do with her body as she pleases. Someone played God and decided what is life and what is a right apart from the Holy Scriptures. The Word of God says that before God formed us in the womb, He knew us and that before we were born, He set us apart. Therefore, we are a soul in the womb, we are a life in the belly. The killing of that life is evil. Our public education does not teach the Word of God in heaven's authoritative form and substance. Why? God-actors decided that the Bible is not good for our children and unlawful for our society. "Don't wear your religion on your sleeve," society says, but that statement just put their belief on their sleeve. The quote is a violent one seeking to push us under the uneven, three-legged couch suffering under the pressure of its weight. At this point, we will be useful only for an empty purpose, a fourth leg. The justifying and cowardly mind says, "The couch needs to be even so I will remain." This mindset only makes oneself feel good about surrendering to evil. Turn the page and flip the couch off you! Living out the truth will make you odd in this lying world. However, if odd gets me to God, then get out of my way. This stand for truth, righteousness, and goodness shows man the way and helps them get in the Way! If society can get you to close your good book, then they will get you to go under the couch as the fourth leg. Not today, Satan! Victory in Jesus!

**2 Corinthians 3:2,3 (KJV) Ye are our epistle written in our hearts, known and read of all men: 3 Forasmuch as ye are manifestly declared to be the epistle of Christ ministered by us, written not with ink, but with the Spirit of the living God; not in tables of stone, but in fleshy tables of the heart.**

**John 1:1 (KJV) In the beginning was the Word, and the Word was with God, and the Word was God.**

**Acts 4:18 (KJV) And they called them, and commanded them not to speak at all nor teach in the name of Jesus.**

# 16. Victory bleeds before victory heals

The glory of the win after the battle is what many imagine in their hearts. The culmination or result of hard work is revealed to the world and rewarded to us. Wait, did you catch that? Hard work. This part of the story is tough to visualize and is overlooked most of the time. Who wants to dream of pain, almost quitting, and the sting of wounds? It is no surprise that the imagination of human nature is glittery and feel-good. Contrary to human nature, it is important to ponder on the pain part and to know how much skin is in the game. I am not speaking of sports with its trophies and medals of metal. I am speaking of triumphing over evil. The attitude and disposition of a person before the battle is where victory begins. The devil asked for blood when he requested trials upon Job. Absorbing a hit to the heart, bandaging wounds, enduring an infirmity of the body, and staring down fear is when your spirit is tested. Praise God for these occasions, for it is important to know the condition of our spirit so we may consciously work to be strengthened. The world says that there are two responses to danger, fight or flight. Both choices align with the flesh. Flight means to run in fear and fight means to be dependent on self's abilities. There is a third option, which is to stand! In the peaceful protests of Dr. Martin Luther King, Jr., he marched, but when the enemies of freedom attacked with violence, he and his fellow protesters, stood. They absorbed the evil even to the point of bloodshed. The result of such a stand melted the hardness of an evil heart and brought healing to a degree that no bullet, fist, or war has ever accomplished. You see, victory bleeds, but it is not another's blood, it is our blood. Jesus shed His blood for us and removed the most dangerous killer in the world, sin! The world wants other people to bleed for their victory, but there is no healing in this scenario because someone will want to avenge the bloodshed. Jesus' bloodshed empowers us to live for Him in victory and overcome when the day of evil visits. Endure your wounds like a good soldier of righteousness. God will heal us. In the healing is strength, for what has been torn down, builds back up stronger. The witnesses of this process will themselves be a part of the healing! Godspeed!

**Philippians 3:10 (KJV) That I may know him, and the power of his resurrection, and the fellowship of his sufferings, being made conformable unto his death;**

**1 John 5:4 (KJV) For whatsoever is born of God overcometh the world: and this is the victory that overcometh the world, even our faith.**

**Ephesians 6:13 (KJV) Wherefore take unto you the whole armour of God, that ye may be able to withstand in the evil day, and having done all, to stand.**

**1 Peter 2:24 (KJV) Who his own self bare our sins in his own body on the tree, that we, being dead to sins, should live unto righteousness: by whose stripes ye were healed.**

# 17. I see the mountain, but soon more and more of it will be under my feet until I see the full sky

Mountains are a wonder of nature that command our attention when in its presence. According to a scientific theory, most mountains are formed through mass movements of the earth's crust or top layer of the earth by its plates colliding and pushing some of those plates upward. This process has not been observed in that no one has seen a mountain just pop out of the ground and grow thousands of feet into the air. So, the roots of a mountain are invisible just like its Maker. The first chapter of Genesis begins by telling us that the earth was without form. The Creator divided the waters under the sky on the third day and brought forth dry land. Then the Lord our God took His artistic hand and shaped the land placing boundaries or coasts, and then created hills, valleys, and mountains. The Lord decided that the highest point on earth would be a mountain named Mount Everest, which is in the Himalayas on the borders of China and Nepal. Many people have perished attempting to reach the summit or top suffering tragedies such as freezing, sickness, avalanches, plummets, and more. A physical mountain is not easy to scale and must be taken on with skill, strength, experience, and good fortune. On a spiritual level, there are trials, attacks, betrayals, and evils that are as big as a mountain. When we first experience a trial or evil our heart sinks and fear grips the soul. This is like first approaching the mountain in awe and seeing oneself as an ant. At a certain moment, we must pray and gather strength from above then use the wisdom of God to place evil under our feet. Every step forward leads up and crushes the enemy down. Mount Everest has guides called Sherpas that aid the ascent up to the summit. The Holy Ghost as well as pastors and spiritual people are our guide on our ascent to the high places. Each spiritual angle of the Lord provides us with the skill, experience, strength, and good fortune to overcome. Once you reach the top and attain the high places the journey will come into perspective. You will realize that God's plan was good and perfect for the strengthening of what was weak. This realization will lead us to a decision to rely on God and increase our faith. Who is like our God? Nobody!

**Psalm 65:5,6 (KJV) By terrible things in righteousness wilt thou answer us, O God of our salvation; who art the confidence of all the ends of the earth, and of them that are afar off upon the sea: 6 Which by his strength setteth fast the mountains; being girded with power:**

**Psalm 36:6 (KJV) Thy righteousness is like the great mountains; thy judgments are a great deep: O Lord, thou preservest man and beast.**

**Psalm 18:33 (KJV) He maketh my feet like hinds' feet, and setteth me upon my high places.**

## 18. In relationships there is unity with God and untying with the devil

The person with all the power, might, and love of all existence wants to have a relationship with us. God designed a long-term relationship with His creation, man. No person, place, or thing can oppose God or compare to His sincere love. With this said, wouldn't it be sensible to enter a relationship with our Heavenly Father due to His abundance of protection, provision, and loving presence? Yes! Unfortunately, the choice of the world is the substitute, the generic, and the decaying relationships. Our choice for relationships such as friends and spouses should be in God and by God with the goal being like our Creator's goal, long-term. A long-term, healthy relationship can only have roots in the doctrines and principles of the Holy Scriptures. Otherwise, there will be fights with permanent and negative damages as well as lasting sadness, which all lead down the paths of death. The relationships apart from God cause evil separations, such as dividing families, breaking up churches, and dissolving friendships. What soul can be saved in a broken church? What heart is content when their family is divided? How much encouragement and support are lost in dissolved friendships? Do not be mistaken, every attack on goodness and love is on purpose and planned in the fires of hell. For God unites, and the devil unties. Open your eyes and fight the real enemy, the venomous Serpent, who separates and takes souls. Though, Satan in no way can take a child of God from the Heavenly Father nor can any person as well. Jesus cannot be taken from you, but our choices can make Him leave. We must with all diligence keep ourselves in the Lord! What about the past or current relationships made apart from God? Well, God can change the substitute, the generic, and the decaying into the long-term, the real, and the flourishing! In the same breath, you may need to walk away too. How do you know what to do? By putting your hand in the hand of the Master. Crying out to the Lord our God and making the relationship with Him the most important of your life. Then step back, watch God step in, and the devil step out! If you have allowed God to work and all you have left is God, then you still have it all! The grace of God be with you. Jesus reigns!

**Proverbs 18:24 (KJV) A man that hath friends must shew himself friendly: and there is a friend that sticketh closer than a brother.**

**Mark 3:25 (KJV) And if a house be divided against itself, that house cannot stand.**

**Romans 16:17 (KJV) Now I beseech you, brethren, mark them which cause divisions and offences contrary to the doctrine which ye have learned; and avoid them.**

**Ephesians 4:3 (KJV) Endeavouring to keep the unity of the Spirit in the bond of peace.**

## 19. The world has me on a lease, for God is my owner

The world has us for a short period. The laughing and mocking ring loud in our ears, but the decibel is dropping every day. The body we occupy along with the body they occupy is made for earth, which is the land of the temporary. Everything and every person have a boundary and time. Where you are and how long you will be there were predetermined. However, how you navigate and where eternity is spent is determined by you. Yes, our soul once brought into existence never ceases to exist. That is the power of the Creator. There are two eternal states our souls will abide in once the temporary fades. The first is with God's love in heaven and the second is with God's wrath in the lake of fire. God has no boundary and has no time. Therefore, God will be everywhere always. I remember being bound by boundaries and giving in to the surrounding environment. I remember being sour by my hour. Then I met Jesus and the wrist lock called a watch was broken off me. My boundary was enlarged on earth and enlarged in God's love! Daily, the enemy seeks to put the lock back on my wrist. Further, Satan seeks to put me back in the boundary I was delivered from. At times, my flesh desires the temporary, the here and now. Enticed by the world, which is the sum of the will of the people who have chosen sin instead of the will of God. The will or consent of the people to sin provides a platform for the devil in most places on earth. That means schools, workplaces, governments, neighborhoods, countries, and so forth have corruption. Even churches and our households become corrupted, so the fight finds us. Do not be dismayed or worn out for the TEMPtations are TEMPorary with God providing rest as needed. The world seeks to bombard us with persecution, mocking, strife, shame, and hate. This is an attempt to make us deny Jesus and lose our place in heaven just like we lost the Garden of Eden. The world believes they can turn our permanent place into a short-lived reservation. Not I said the fly! I belong to God, I belong to love, joy, and peace in the Holy Ghost forever! Glory to the Most High God, El Elyon!

**2 Corinthians 4:18 (KJV) While we look not at the things which are seen, but at the things which are not seen: for the things which are seen are temporal; but the things which are not seen are eternal.**

**Acts 17:26,27 (KJV) And hath made of one blood all nations of men for to dwell on all the face of the earth, and hath determined the times before appointed, and the bounds of their habitation; 27 That they should seek the Lord, if haply they might feel after him, and find him, though he be not far from every one of us:**

**Galatians 6:8 (KJV) For he that soweth to his flesh shall of the flesh reap corruption; but he that soweth to the Spirit shall of the Spirit reap life everlasting.**

## 20. God is ever-present, hearing when we confess our sins, and hearing when we plan our sins

One unique distinction between a child and an adult is that a child reveals their motives while an adult hides them. A child lets you know that they do not want to share, but an adult will give you something with a smile while being bitter in their heart about giving you that something. We are not fooling God though. He knows our motives. This brings us to the age-old philosophical question. If a tree falls in the forest, does it make a sound? Some say no because a sound exists only when someone hears it thus deeming it a sound. While others say yes, regardless of someone being there to witness the sound and call it a sound. Well, adults do not realize that there is a witness, a listener who hears the thoughts of our hearts and mind. God is the hearer and witness. He makes all matters official in His presence! If a man sins in the forest with no one there, is he getting away with it? No. When a person has a need, he raises awareness to God so that he may be heard. Somehow, during times of lust and sin, a person goes through the steps of hiding and covering, thinking that God will not be aware. Whether we try to get God's attention or out of His attention, He is omnipresent or always present. The wise choice is to be aware of God, to be spirit-conscience, and obey His Word day and night. This will make for a short confession and a long blessing! I say short confession because we will always wrestle with the flesh, this earth-conscience body, that wants to obey the lusts thereof. Ever-present should not be taken as a negative. Why do children carry a blanket or stuffed animal with them wherever they go? This is for comfort and company. We are never alone. Our carnal mind and emotions may not feel it, or should I say feel Him, but the Holy Ghost is with us. If we continue in faith God always shows himself. Soon, it will be realized that even when we thought He was not there, He was there in a bigger way! This happens in sin as well. We think that we are getting away with it and false comfort sets in with overconfidence. Some believe God is even allowing sin, but this is far from the truth, and it is a lie, a deception. God never allows sin, nor does He ever plan for us to sin. Mercy and grace will be extended in the form of a rebuke, which may come gently or harshly depending on our level of knowledge of sin. Be mindful of the Lord our God and plan to be a servant to righteousness. Blessed be the Name of the Lord!

**Proverbs 20:11 (KJV) Even a child is known by his doings, whether his work be pure, and whether it be right.**

**Proverbs 23:7 (KJV) For as he thinketh in his heart, so is he: Eat and drink, saith he to thee; but his heart is not with thee.**

**Proverbs 15:3 (KJV) The eyes of the Lord are in every place, beholding the evil and the good.**

**Jeremiah 17:10 (KJV) I the Lord search the heart, I try the reins, even to give every man according to his ways, and according to the fruit of his doings.**

# 21. I accept your words better than trophies

Most professional sports are played for a championship that is represented by a trophy. The trophy symbolizes victory and informs the world of what and who deserves praise. Let us not forget that vast amounts of financial incentives are involved that reward the players, coaches, and owners. This sums up what the pride of a person desires, public praise and profit. This put in plain words is a person desiring a reward for his work. This same principle comes into play morally as well when a man does charitable work or any good deed, he must be acknowledged and/or rewarded. When the rich ruler approached Jesus and said that He was a good master, Jesus deflected or redirected his praise to above saying, "There is none good but one, that is, God." How interesting since Jesus is God! Our Lord is making a minimum of two points. The first is that although Jesus is good, in His bodily form He is dependent on God to do good or for good to go through Him. The second point was to create awareness to the rich ruler that his mindset of good was not spiritual or according to God's will. What Jesus did accept was the title of Master, which is a teacher who is a master in his learning and instruction especially with scripture, God, and the duties of man. This was His proper title and who He was because Jesus grew, which means labored or worked in His bodily form to reach maturity in the knowledge of God. Therefore, I take on this attitude of Christ and I do my best for others to see God by my good deeds. Therefore, for any good that comes through me that impacts someone to the point of them expressing words to me, I accept it better than trophies. I accept the proper label of a disciple of God while also directing praise to our Heavenly Father, who is the origin of all good! There are no stadiums of praise, there is just a person with a sincere heart overflowing with thanks. This makes my heart overflow with thanks to God! The attitude of Christ seeks no profit or substance increase, just love. Jesus revealed to the rich ruler where he lacked, which was that he trusted in his possessions and not in God. In other words, he lived for the trophies. How much reward belongs to a man for a good deed? The reward of love! When we love with the attitude of Christ, we are then God's trophy!

**Luke 18:18-30 Story of the rich ruler**

**Matthew 6:2 (KJV) Therefore when thou doest thine alms, do not sound a trumpet before thee, as the hypocrites do in the synagogues and in the streets, that they may have glory of men. Verily I say unto you, They have their reward.**

**Philippians 2:13 (KJV) For it is God which worketh in you both to will and to do of his good pleasure.**

**Matthew 5:16 (KJV) Let your light so shine before men, that they may see your good works, and glorify your Father which is in heaven.**

## 22. The glory is not at the top; it is higher with Jesus!

In this secular world the higher you go the more isolated a person gets from family, friends, and genuine experiences. I recall a story in which a CEO resigned his position after he reflected on how much time he lost with his daughter. This is the Babylonian way, the way of seeking success and wealth without understanding, humbleness, and God. Its design is to destroy a soul, making it so lost until the expiration of that soul's time. That is when the big hand of God will reap what was sown, death unto the evildoer and life unto the righteous. People and even "believers," seem to forget the greatest commandment, which is to love the Lord our God with all our heart, mind, soul, and strength. Therefore, the goals and ambitions of this world should come secondary. Trust in God with the timing and execution of His plan for our lives. My father, Pastor James Arevalo, would share a common joke about himself. He would joke that he was a doctor because he is a Ph.D., post-hole digger. Everyone would crack up and laugh. One day, my father was recommended for a Doctor of Divinity. He applied, fulfilled the submission requirements, and went under review. My father was granted an honorary Doctor of Divinity. Now, he is Dr. James Arevalo! He aimed for Jesus, not the top, and still made it there! In the process, many souls were blessed and provided with the Gospel of Jesus Christ because he lived by faith and put God first! Does the world succeed or make it to the top without God? Yes and no. Yes, because God still blesses them with talent and inspiration, but they are using God without acknowledging Him. God allows this because of free will, but we will give an account on judgment day of how we used our talents. No, the world does not succeed because they are not wise enough to admit to themselves and others of the help God provides consequently not giving due honor where it is deserved. When a person succeeds without God, love does not win. Every accomplishment must be in honor of God to truly succeed. That is when the Gospel is given its place and salvation is nearer. Aim to use your talents to bring you and others to God. Glory to the Son over glory for one because glory for the Son means glory for everyone! Hallelujah!

**1 Samuel 2:30 (KJV) Wherefore the Lord God of Israel saith, I said indeed that thy house, and the house of thy father, should walk before me for ever: but now the Lord saith, Be it far from me; for them that honour me I will honour, and they that despise me shall be lightly esteemed.**

**1 Corinthians 9:26 (KJV) I therefore so run, not as uncertainly; so fight I, not as one that beateth the air:**

**Philippians 2:3 (KJV) Let nothing be done through strife or vainglory; but in lowliness of mind let each esteem other better than themselves.**

**Daniel 12:3 (KJV) And they that be wise shall shine as the brightness of the firmament; and they that turn many to righteousness as the stars for ever and ever.**

## 23. Like the moon in the morning, I survive the night and become one with the Son

The moon borrows its light from the sun, which makes it visible throughout the night. Early in the morning, the moon can still be seen, but as the sun comes up more, the sunlight envelopes the moon. The light is an accurate depiction of God's presence, which gives us life in the valley of the shadow of death. The moon is an accurate depiction of us, needing and borrowing God's presence for aid through the night or the darkness of evil. When we perfect our walk in the Lord and learn how to be full of the Holy Ghost then we become enveloped in the light of God! God started us off as dirt of the earth. The dust we did breathe and consume until the cross between heaven and earth appeared to us. Then what was clay, brittle, and limited was filled with holy fire that baked and shaped a new creation. It's amazing to be created and even greater to be newly created for God's purpose. A purpose of life, love, and pure beauty. Look at God's sun and see its brilliance and power, which heats and ignites life on earth. The sun is not visible in the night, but its evidence remains. We cannot physically see God right now, but He is working, putting effort into igniting eternal life for His children. Look at God's moon, which is in place to guide the sojourners of the night. According to science, the moon also helps in stabilizing the climate of the earth. What an analogy, for the power of God that passes through our lives helps stabilize the world! You see God's purposes are massive yet filled with the most intricate of details. Therefore, without God we cannot understand, we cannot hold knowledge, and we cannot exercise wisdom. Very plainly, we can do nothing that lasts for an eternity. You may say, the sun and the moon are temporary, but its speech is not. Its message is that there is a God, a God who made it for you. Further, the speech proclaims that God is intelligent, gigantic, and beyond the universe, yet reaching you where you live. What is your speech? What do you proclaim? Will your message last for an eternity? If you become one with the Son your impact will be eternal. Our light will never be extinguished. While Jesus was on the earth He said, I and the Father are one! Blessed be the name of the Lord!

**Deuteronomy 33:14 (KJV) And for the precious fruits brought forth by the sun, and for the precious things put forth by the moon**

**Psalm 19:4 (KJV) Their line is gone out through all the earth, and their words to the end of the world. In them hath he set a tabernacle for the sun**

**Psalm 8:3 (KJV) When I consider thy heavens, the work of thy fingers, the moon and the stars, which thou hast ordained**

**John 15:5 (KJV) I am the vine, ye are the branches: He that abideth in me, and I in him, the same bringeth forth much fruit: for without me ye can do nothing.**

# 24. Focus on the Maker, not the mocker!

When a person is fouled in basketball that person earns the right to take free throw shots. These are shots taken without any defense from the opposing team, but this does not stop the crowd from distracting. The crowd will scream, move arms around, or utilize any distractive antic to break the focus of the shooter. Wait, so the free throw shooter was fouled and earned the free throws, yet the crowd still roots against the shooter? Ladies and gentlemen welcome to the mocker's world! A righteous person lives with sacrifice, purity, and persecution. The righteous swallow their pride and do their best to love and strive to make peace with all men. The righteous earn the right to be heard, honored, and respected. These attributes do not stop the mocker from scorning or belittling the righteous. When the righteous put on the armor of God, the opposing team which is demons and devils must abide by the rules of engagement dictated by heaven. The mocker is the crowd who scoffs at rules and engages with lawlessness attempting to distract. I think it is fitting that in Psalm 1 the Word of God says not to SIT in the seat of the scornful a/k/a mocker. Sitting at times can be considered a lazy and self-indulged posture. While sitting, the mocker in pride demeans the efforts of the righteous. I have witnessed that the strongest mocker is the weakest person. Since the mocker knows the righteous choose not to fight back, they turn up the heat and take advantage. This makes the blood boil! The righteous are not completely defenseless though, for there are weapons and strategies, just not carnal ones! It can be very upsetting to be provoked by mockery and our old, unsaved person wants to foul someone. Thank God for coach Holy Ghost who redirects our focus. When you focus on the Maker, Jesus, that is when perspective is broadened. The communication from heaven to the soul paints the picture of our Savior. Jesus walked the earth, endured the lies, and mockery to save us. How cruel of the world to strike Jesus then ask Him in mockery to prophesy who threw the strike. Jesus' example should bring us to reflection and recall that we were the mocker at one time. It just wasn't the Roman soldiers who struck Jesus, it was our sin. We must forgive and be filled with warmth and love, which redirects our focus to the goal of the fight. The goal is salvation for us and others! Look up, focus, love, then......Swish! That's a point for God's team!

**Jude 1:18 (KJV) How that they told you there should be mockers in the last time, who should walk after their own ungodly lusts.**

**Proverbs 21:24 (KJV) Proud and haughty scorner is his name, who dealeth in proud wrath**

**Isaiah 26:3 (KJV) Thou wilt keep him in perfect peace, whose mind is stayed on thee: because he trusteth in thee.**

**Luke 6:32 (KJV) For if ye love them which love you, what thank have ye? for sinners also love those that love them.**

## 25. Souls want the blessings, but do not want to be the blessed!

On the streets, it is said that to be the boss you must pay the cost. To move higher there has got to be groundwork, hustle, and grit. Further, there are prices to pay as well, such as the burden of major decisions. Many people seek to bypass the groundwork and hope to relish in the perks or benefits of a boss only. Perks like handing out orders, feeling important, financial gain, and receiving praise. This is a trap indeed that is sure to create chaos because a higher position not merited or earned will lack righteous abilities. So, a person wants the perks without the works! If you did not go through the oppression, then more than likely you will become the oppressor. How could a person understand the burden of the work requested if they never did the work? This is just human nature, unable to understand most of the time without referencing self. That is why Jesus said to do to others as you would have them do to you. In the church today there is a negative trend. Souls want the blessings, but do not want to pay the cost to be the blessed. People will at times seek God only for the perks. Generally, a situation is driving this person like a debt, sickness, needing comfort through a trial, and so forth. Once the situation is reduced or goes away, then a person is no longer motivated to seek God and be a part of the church. This can be called being a convenient seeker of the Lord. A convenient seeker of the Lord sticks around in church throughout the situation so that the blessed folk will bless them with financial support, comfort, healing, and so forth. You see, the blessed folk, have their blessings because they have gone through their trials and earned favor from God. A convenient seeker of God moves in and out to absorb the blessings only. When another situation arises, the cycle is repeated. Oh, and we can't forget that when they leave, a convenient seeker falsely blames and shames the blessed thus completing their enter and exit strategy. So, they want the perks without the works! Woe unto them that do such evil! God bless the blessed folk who endure the cycles to eventually win over the soul to Jesus! In this world everything costs, so pay the price for righteousness because there is no better investment, return, and reward! Glory unto the Lamb of God!

**Romans 16:18 (KJV) For they that are such serve not our Lord Jesus Christ, but their own belly; and by good words and fair speeches deceive the hearts of the simple.**

**1 John 2:19 (KJV) They went out from us, but they were not of us; for if they had been of us, they would no doubt have continued with us: but they went out, that they might be made manifest that they were not all of us.**

**1 Timothy 5:18 (KJV) For the scripture saith, thou shalt not muzzle the ox that treadeth out the corn. And, The labourer is worthy of his reward.**

**Luke 6:28 (KJV) Bless them that curse you, and pray for them which despitefully use you**

## 26. When does life begin? Easy solve, ask the Creator, easy fail, ask the created.

No one has seen the beginning of life and the end of life while they walk the earth. Further, every man is limited and cannot know everything, nor experience everything. As a result, using science to answer the beginning and end of life or afterlife will always be a partial answer. It all boils down to faith! Isn't this what God said throughout the Bible, faith? Yes! Mankind says religion is flawed and just fills in gaps, but what about the gaps of evolution that get filled by guesses? Evolution is still a debate, yet it is accepted as law, truth, and supremacy. It is forced by penalty of law (in public schools), and social punishments like mockery and ostracizing. Hmmm, this does not follow the scientific community's narrative of being tolerant, unforceful, and cordial. People say science is harmless, yet it created the atomic bomb, which can kill thousands in a single detonation. Man is a created being. His science is convenient and allowed to fail without consequences from society. If his science is wrong, he just says, "Oops, I am still learning." Then the theory gets revised, but a revision with a deeper deception. When a believer in evolution faces God on judgment day, what can they say, "I believed an unproven and debatable theory was the truth?" This is not going to work. I challenge you to sincerely ask God, our Creator, to introduce Himself to you. I know without any doubt God will answer you! The Creator has given us the answer in Jesus! Prophesied, testified, verified, and certified repeatedly throughout time, space, and the human experience. What the Holy Bible says comes to pass or proves true whether it is followed on purpose, by accident, or by deliberate contradiction. Specifically, the life, death, and resurrection of Jesus uproots all lies and forever plants the tree of truth. Truth was in action when Jesus came to the earth and no person has had such a profound impact on the earth. Man's narrative about the beginning of life has changed countless times, but God's narrative remains the same, "In the beginning, God created the heavens and the earth." Ask the Creator! Praise in the Highest to God!

**Hebrews 11:3 (KJV) Through faith we understand that the worlds were framed by the word of God, so that things which are seen were not made of things which do appear.**

**Romans 3:4 (KJV) God forbid: yea, let God be true, but every man a liar; as it is written, That thou mightest be justified in thy sayings, and mightest overcome when thou art judged.**

**John 5:39 (KJV) Search the scriptures; for in them ye think ye have eternal life: and they are they which testify of me.**

**Revelation 1:8 (KJV) I am Alpha and Omega, the beginning and the ending, saith the Lord, which is, and which was, and which is to come, the Almighty.**

# 27. I am man's second pick, but God's first pick

A phone call comes in explaining to me that I did not receive the job. Another phone call comes in about two weeks later explaining that I am now being offered the job because the first pick did not work out. What the interviewer did not see in me the first time is a mystery. What I do know is that God knew who I was the first time and reserved me to eventually obtain the position the second time. Now, let's translate this principle to Christians and their interaction with the world. I have observed Christians be the second pick in friendships, invitations to events, honorable mentions, and so forth. Then when the storm or a hard time comes, the Christian becomes the pick. This has been confirmed by the picker themselves. I have heard the confessions of, "You're the first person that came to mind," and "I knew you were the only person that could help." At the fun things and honorable things, the Christian is overlooked. This happens because the world knows that they have the Christian's love, so they pander or please the fake persons to gain their love. Deep inside the picker's heart, they know who is truly reliable. This is a travesty or sham of a friendship or relationship. It is using people, in this case, Christians, while allowing themselves (pickers) to be abused by fake persons. Wow, what an injustice, evil depravity! Praise be to God for the victory though! God has a way of moving Christians to the seat of honor and at times doing so without any efforts on a Christian's part. However, Christians do not seek this when they do what they do. For Christians, the reward is in sharing the love of Christ. Christ was the second pick for the world. The world needs to realize that for its biggest problem, sin, Christ is the first and only pick. That is why when the pickers a/k/a world, yelled crucify Him, Jesus said, "Forgive them for they know not what they do." If we please God, man will come to the full realization later. Until then, do not be offended at the second pick, but be in fear and gratitude to be God's first pick. Be worshiped forever, Lord!

**Luke 6:22 (KJV) Blessed are ye, when men shall hate you, and when they shall separate you from their company, and shall reproach you, and cast out your name as evil, for the Son of man's sake.**

**Daniel 5:12 (KJV) Forasmuch as an excellent spirit, and knowledge, and understanding, interpreting of dreams, and shewing of hard sentences, and dissolving of doubts, were found in the same Daniel, whom the king named Belteshazzar: now let Daniel be called, and he will shew the interpretation.**

**Matthew 27:17,21 (KJV) Therefore when they were gathered together, Pilate said unto them, Whom will ye that I release unto you? Barabbas, or Jesus which is called Christ? 21 The governor answered and said unto them, Whether of the twain will ye that I release unto you? They said, Barabbas.**

# 28. To not fear death, one must fully live in faith for Christ

The greatest fear of man is death. A man would rather live in punishment than face death. This is evident in criminal death penalty cases wherein the convicted works to commute or change the sentence from death to life imprisonment. There is a minority of people who do choose to end their lives themselves, but it is still fear that this person has chosen. The devil deceives them by instilling in them a fear of living and the lie that there is nothing after death. I am always amazed at the fight for life in the insect world. No matter how injured an insect is the bug will continue to fight until the last breath. What does an insect know about life that makes it fight so hard? This is a beautiful example from our Lord! The life we live in the body is great, even though it comes with consequences. So, if being born is great what does being born again mean? It means to reach the fullness of life, which is the spiritual substance of our existence. God is spirit and a person can communicate and feel the fullness of God, such as love, joy, and peace by being spiritual! Here is the kicker, to become a spiritual person one must repent of their sins done in and as a fleshly body. Crucify our flesh so that our spirit lives forever. What stops a person from repenting? Pride, lusts of eyes, the lust of the flesh, and ironically fear. Fear kills. Life is given through faith! Faith that knows Jesus died for our sins and that He resurrected from the dead. Faith that knows the life we live in obedience pleases an invisible God. Faith that knows that death is only the beginning of life! Living for Christ is choosing great over small, truth over lies, and eternity over temporary. So, in essence, our pride and lusts die daily preparing us for the final battle of the spirit leaving the corruptible body to take on the incorruptible body. If internally a person can choose death to the fleshly nature by the power of the blood of Christ, then externally facing death is just a testimony for the world to see and hear. What a person experiences by crucifying the flesh is pure freedom for the reason that they are not a slave to desires, addictions, sorrow, anger, and so on. When a person is spiritual then God is the head and liberty reigns. A person who is in the flesh is subject to fear. A person in the spirit is subject to faith. What and who is your master? Come, Lord Jesus, come!

**Hebrews 2:15 (KJV) And deliver them who through fear of death were all their lifetime subject to bondage.**

**Matthew 8:26 (KJV) And he saith unto them, Why are ye fearful, O ye of little faith? Then he arose, and rebuked the winds and the sea; and there was a great calm.**

**Philippians 1:21 (KJV) For to me to live is Christ, and to die is gain.**

**Hebrews 11:27 (KJV) By faith he forsook Egypt, not fearing the wrath of the king: for he endured, as seeing him who is invisible.**

# 29. Do not fear the heights of raising the standard

Status quo is when all persons in a particular gathering agree to interact by certain rules. A gathering or group of people can be illustrated as follows; job, party, public events, family interaction, and basically when people agree to meet with other people. Here is a note, most gatherings and groups do not abide by the rules of the Bible and are secular or of the world. There is neutral ground, but the lines are drawn with the smallest of margins so be cautious. When the rules are followed in a particular group there is smooth operation, and all seem to get along. Two things plague groups due to the flaws of human nature when it comes to rules. One, as the group progresses the rules become more liberal and at times what was forbidden becomes acceptable. Two, when a person in a group has morals that conflict with the group then that person is met with pressure. The pressure to either conform or to speak and act against the group. This is where the fear sets in for a person having a conviction to do the right thing, for this person knows the consequences. The consequences could mean loss of pay, loss of friendship, loss of family members, feelings of hurt, and any type of negative stress. These consequences are the group's way of punishing the dissident or nonconformist for not doing what they want.  It is a violent tactic. This is a challenge especially for a believer because we always raise the group's moral standards. The standard is the highest, the Word of God! Even though you are doing what is best for the group, they are still blinded by the flaws of human nature, which are preyed upon by demons. That is right, it is a spiritual battle! You see, you raise the standard to testify of the One who made the raised standard, the God of Abraham, Isaac, and Jacob! This is what the men and women of faith in the Bible were known for since they would not compromise with the world even upon pain or death. What should be on our minds and in our hearts is the conviction to please God no matter the outcome. Do not fear, embrace the challenge, and show how the rules lead to the Ruler, Jesus Christ! Praise God, thank God!

1 Peter 4:4 (KJV) Wherein they think it strange that ye run not with them to the same excess of riot, speaking evil of you:

Ephesians 5:11 (KJV) And have no fellowship with the unfruitful works of darkness, but rather reprove them.

John 15:19 (KJV) If ye were of the world, the world would love his own: but because ye are not of the world, but I have chosen you out of the world, therefore the world hateth you.

Titus 1:9 (KJV) Holding fast the faithful word as he hath been taught, that he may be able by sound doctrine both to exhort and to convince the gainsayers.

# 30. The mind is a mirror to the Lord, from the limitless comes limitless

What builds cities, structures, and civilizes the earth utilizing its resources? What invents, has technological advances, and masters mathematics and the sciences? The mind of man! No creation does more with its mind than man. It is this mind, consciousness (self-aware) and conscience (moral code), that separates us from the animals. If an animal and man share similar brain structures, how does man receive his consciousness? This mystery baffles science since a mind comes from meat or flesh. So, for thousands of years, our mind has had trouble understanding itself. Here is the short answer, the mind comes from God, birth the moment His breath filled our nostrils from the dust. What power God placed in us and even bestowed upon us the honor of being made in His image, His likeness! The mind processes all stimuli from the earth to interpret harm and safety. The mind weighs moral dilemmas to determine good and evil. These intricate methods can boil down to a simple, yes and no. Does God exist? Yes! Do thorns prick? Yes. Can you touch fire? No. There is beauty in the details and beauty in the simple. Some of the choices are temporary, like eating to not be hungry. Some of the choices are permanent, like having children. An eternal soul exists in a temporary body. When we go to sleep, the mind is supposed to shut down, but something in us stays awake or just keeps going. Another example is math, do numbers stop or can you keep counting limitlessly? My little sister said this one day, "Jesus is the number that does not stop!"

I was blown away by this notion. There are eternal properties in the temporary world, which is us seeing the mirror view of the real thing! Why? It is the breadcrumbs that lead to the Bread of Life, Jesus! Jesus is the ultimate Yes! A yes that will be limitless in rest, joy, peace, and all that is good. You cannot wrap your mind around it, you can only feel the confirmation in your soul from the Holy Ghost. You know that you know you are saved and will be counted among the righteous. Let your mind reflect above! May God be praised limitlessly!

**Hebrews 8:10 (KJV) For this is the covenant that I will make with the house of Israel after those days, saith the Lord; I will put my laws into their mind, and write them in their hearts: and I will be to them a God, and they shall be to me a people:**

**2 Corinthians 11:3 (KJV) But I fear, lest by any means, as the serpent beguiled Eve through his subtilty, so your minds should be corrupted from the simplicity that is in Christ.**

**2 Corinthians 1:20 (KJV) For all the promises of God in him are yea, and in him Amen, unto the glory of God by us.**

**1 Corinthians 2:16 (KJV) For who hath known the mind of the Lord, that he may instruct him? but we have the mind of Christ.**

# 31. Why is the humble man stronger because he can lift others above himself

Choosing pride does not make you strong, it just makes you one person effective, which is not love. The self-narrative of pride is a lie, which affects or influences self and others negatively. For example, when someone strikes our cheek why does God command us to turn the other cheek? The reasons why are that consistently to stop violence it must be met with peace, and human nature through pride wants to strike back. Why does pride want to strike back? Pride does not want to be shamed or humbled, does not know how to handle pain, and is just looking out for self-interest. The self-interest of punishing someone for not giving our perceived importance. Imagine Jesus being one person effective when He was falsely accused and sought for arrest. Jesus informed the disciples that He could pray for more than twelve legions of angels, implying that He could crush His enemies. Yet, Jesus did not do this because He said that the scriptures needed to be fulfilled instead. Jesus was strong enough to endure the shame and to choose to be humble for the saving of many. When we humble and choose to turn the other cheek, wood is taken out of the fire of violence. At this moment humbleness is lifting love, peace, and the Holy Scriptures as of the utmost importance. Further, the striker or attacker is being helped and valued even though they are not aware. Helped and valued because the strike is absorbed, and the shame is absorbed for their good too. All these things lifted above self to labor for the greater good! There is a reason why

God had to illustrate humbleness in the Holy Scriptures because He knows our prideful nature. God has every right and privilege to command humbleness because He humbled from the highest point of existence, the throne of heaven, to the lowest point of existence, pits of hell, to save souls. Further, just as the cross was lifted high, so was the worth of man, the love for his soul, and the desire for God to have an everlasting relationship with His children. Therefore, God and His Word deserve to be fulfilled and lifted above pride. Is satisfying oneself worth all the chaos and destruction that comes from it? Who are we to play God and make our own rules? Let go of the weakness of not being able to suffer. Humble thyself and lift others and love. Then God shall lift you! Thank you, Heavenly Father!

**Proverbs 13:10 (KJV) Only by pride cometh contention: but with the well advised is wisdom.**

**Proverbs 29:23 (KJV) A man's pride shall bring him low: but honour shall uphold the humble in spirit.**

**Matthew 20:26 (KJV) But it shall not be so among you: but whosoever will be great among you, let him be your minister**

**Philippians 2:8 (KJV) And being found in fashion as a man, he humbled himself, and became obedient unto death, even the death of the cross.**

# ACKNOWLEDGMENTS

I would like to express my gratitude to my children and family for their sincere support of this book. I am thankful to Miracle Harvest Church for their love and prayers! Honorary recognition to my sister Ariel for creating the cover art from my mind as well as helping brainstorm the design. Esteem recognition to my sister Adley for brainstorming, resourcefulness, reading book, typography work, and support. Special recognition to my sister Crystal for being the first to read this book as well as proofreading and editing suggestions. I also thank my family in advance for the marketing, distribution efforts, and positive declarations of this book! Thank you to anyone who reads this book! Thank you to anyone who recommends this book! I love you and Jesus loves you! Thank you, Jesus, for your unconditional love and support! Your love O Lord brings life from death, positive from negative, and joy from despair! Who is like you? No one!

**I can do all things through Christ which strengtheneth me. Philippians 4:13 (KJV)**

# How to Contact

Please visit miracleharvestministries.com to connect with church services, donate to the ministry, and stay updated on outreaches

Follow Miracle Harvest Ministries on Facebook and Instagram

Please visit reverbnation.com/holytunes for free Christian hip-hop music downloads

Follow Holy Tunes a/k/a Weeping Prophet on Facebook, Instagram, and Snapchat

To book Co-Pastor Jeremiah Arevalo for speaking/preaching engagements, testimonial, and hip-hop ministry you may contact the above Facebook messengers or email at

jeremiah.phil413@gmail.com

Made in the USA
Coppell, TX
15 March 2022

74923141R00039